S.H.A.P.E.

FINDING & FULFILLING YOUR UNIQUE
PURPOSE FOR LIFE

D0730825

ERIK REES

WITH FOREWORD BY RICK WARREN

SMALL GROUP STUDY GUIDE

Published by Purpose Driven® Publishing

PurposeDriven®

20 Empire
Lake Forest, CA 92630
www.purposedriven.com

TABLE OF CONTENTS

FOREWORD

by Rick Warren
Author of *The Purpose Driven® Life*

God has given every creature he made a special area of expertise to fulfill its purpose. For instance, some animals run, others hop, some swim, others burrow, and some fly. Each has a particular role to play based on the way they were shaped by God. This is equally true of you and every other human being. You were uniquely designed, wired, and "shaped" by God to do certain things. You are not an assembly-line product, mass produced without any thought. You are a custom-designed, one-of-a-kind, original masterpiece.

In my book, *The Purpose Driven® Life*, I introduced the concept of "S.H.A.P.E.," a simple acrostic I created more than twenty years ago to help people remember five factors God uses to prepare and equip us for our purpose in life. These five shaping tools are our Spiritual gifts, Heart, Abilities, Personality, and Experiences. You are shaped to serve God by serving others.

Now, in this wonderful, long-needed group study series, presented by Erik Rees, we take a more thorough, in-depth look at the implications and applications of S.H.A.P.E. Erik has served by my side at Saddleback Church for ten years. As our pastor of ministry, his job is to help people in our church family discover their S.H.A.P.E., find their niche, and experience the joy of being what God created them to be. He is passionate about helping people unlock their God-given potential, and I can say without any reservation that Erik understands more about helping you discern and develop your S.H.A.P.E. than any other person on the planet.

Before architects design any new building, they first ask, "What will be its purpose? How will it be used?" The intended function always determines the form of the building. Before God created you, he decided what role he wanted you to play on earth. He planned exactly how he wanted you to serve him, and then he shaped you for those tasks. You are the way you are because you were made for a specific contribution on earth.

God never wastes anything. He would not give you abilities, interests, talents, gifts, personality, and life experiences unless he intended to use them for his glory. By identifying and understanding these factors, you can discover God's will for your life. I can guarantee that you are going to benefit from this focus on S.H.A.P.E. discovery in an incredible way.

With more than thirty million readers of *The Purpose Driven® Life*, we are now seeing a movement of purpose driven people around the world who are embracing and expressing their unique shape in serving God and mankind. I invite you to join us in this movement!

Let us know what you are discovering, and how you are using your S.H.A.P.E. We'd love to hear from you. E-mail your story to us at ***shape@purposedriven.com***. I'm excited about how much you are going to grow!

A MESSAGE FROM THE AUTHOR

I'm so glad you are reading this. That means you and your small group are about to embark on an amazing journey with Jesus. This expedition promises to help each of you begin to understand who God made you to be, so you can discover what he made you to do for him with your life on earth.

Before you start, please note that this curriculum was designed as a complementary resource to my book, *S.H.A.P.E.: Finding and Fulfilling Your Unique Purpose for Life*. Over the next six weeks I will personally guide you through key content from the book's first six chapters.

The "Diving Deeper" sections at the end of each study guide session direct you to additional reading from the book. This reading, plus the online assessment tools, deepens your understanding and assists you in unlocking your God-given S.H.A.P.E. Together, these resources help clarify all God has given you to serve him, and show you how your S.H.A.P.E. defines your unique purpose for life.

I truly hope you and your group have a great time of study and service to God.

Blessings,

Erik Rees
Pastor of S.H.A.P.E. & Serving
Saddleback Church

UNDERSTANDING YOUR STUDY GUIDE

Here is a brief explanation of the features of this study guide.

Looking Ahead / Catching Up: You will open each meeting with an opportunity for everyone to check in with each other about how you are doing with the weekly assignments. Accountability is a key to success in this study!

Key Verse: Each week you will find a key verse or Scripture passage for your group to read together. If someone in the group has a different translation, ask them to read it aloud so the group can get a bigger picture of the meaning of the passage.

Video Lesson: There is a fifteen-minute video lesson for the group to watch together each week. Fill in the blanks in the lesson outlines as you watch the video, and be sure to refer back to these outlines during your discussion time.

Discussion Questions: Each video segment is complemented by several questions for group discussion. Please don't feel pressured to discuss every single question. The material in this study is meant to be your servant, not your master. So there is no reason to rush through the answers. Give everyone ample opportunity to share their thoughts. If you don't get through all of the discussion questions, that's OK.

Living on Purpose: In his book, *The Purpose Driven Life*, Rick Warren identifies God's five purposes for our lives. They are worship, fellowship, discipleship, ministry, and evangelism. We will focus on one or two of these five purposes in each lesson, and discuss how they relate to the subject of the study. This section is very important, so please be sure to leave time for it.

Prayer Direction: At the end of each session you will find suggestions for your group prayer time. Praying together is one of the greatest privileges of small group life. Please don't take it for granted.

Putting It into Practice: This is where the rubber meets the road. We don't want to be just hearers of the Word. We also need to be doers of the Word (James 1:22). This section of the study explains the assignments we would like you to complete before your next meeting. These assignments are application exercises that will help you put into practice the truths you have discussed in the lesson.

Diving Deeper: The material in this small group study is designed to complement the book, *S.H.A.P.E.: Finding and Fulfilling Your Unique Purpose for Life*, by Erik Rees (Zondervan, 2006). While reading the book is not a required component of this study, this section will direct you to additional reading from the book for greater understanding of the topic.

As your group is forming and getting ready to begin this journey together, it's important to identify one person who will fill the role of ministry champion.

MINISTRY CHAMPION:

The Role

The ministry champion works with everyone in the group, either collectively or one-on-one, to make sure everyone is on track with the study. This role does not require any professional skills, just a heart for the spiritual growth of others. The ministry champion's role is also to help each group member clarify their unique, God-given S.H.A.P.E., and begin to express it within the group.

The Responsibilities

Help every group member:

- Discover their God-given S.H.A.P.E.

- Define their unique Kingdom Purpose

- Develop their ninety-day ministry action plan

- Determine great ways for the entire small group to serve God together

S.H.A.P.E.

HOW TO USE THIS VIDEO CURRICULUM

Follow these four simple steps for a successful small group meeting:

1. Open your group meeting by using the "Looking Ahead" or "Catching Up" sections of your study guide.

2. Watch the video lesson together and take notes in the outlines in this study guide. Each video lesson is between fifteen and twenty minutes in length.

3. Complete the rest of the discussion materials for each session, including the "Living on Purpose" and "Prayer Direction" sections.

4. Review the "Putting It into Practice" assignments and commit to doing them before your next meeting.

SESSION
ONE

ONLY YOU
CAN BE YOU

DISCOVERING WHAT YOU
ARE DESIGNED TO DO

LOOKING AHEAD

- If your group is new or your have new members, take a few minutes to let everyone introduce themselves and share how they came to be part of this group.

- Share with the group why you are here. What is the one thing you want God to do in your life as a result of this study?

- Here at the beginning of your journey, how would you define a life purpose, or a life contribution?

KEY VERSE

Make a careful exploration of who you are and the work you have been given, and then sink yourself into that. Don't be impressed with yourself. Don't compare yourself with others. Each of you must take responsibility for doing the creative best you can with your own life.

Galatians 6:4–5 (MSG)

Watch the Session One video now and fill in the blanks in the outline in this guide. Refer back to the outline during your discussion time.

ONLY YOU CAN BE YOU

For we are God's masterpiece. He has created us anew in Christ Jesus, so that we can do the good things he planned for us long ago.

(Ephesians 2:10 NLT)

Your journey to discover your S.H.A.P.E. begins with an honest question: *Who am I?*

- You have a specific purpose in life . . . a special assignment from God that only you can accomplish.

- It's what Pastor Rick Warren calls "your life contribution."

"What will be the _____ of my life?"

Your Kingdom Purpose:

Your specific contribution to the body of Christ, within your generation, that causes you to totally_____ on God and authentically _____ his love toward others—all through the expression of your uniqueness.

Most people define their purpose in life by:

1. _____

2. What others _____them

3. God's _____

S.H.A.P.E.

S.H.A.P.E. OVERVIEW

> Whenever God gives us an assignment, he always equips us with what we need to accomplish it. This custom combination of capabilities is called your S.H.A.P.E.
>
> —Rick Warren, *The Purpose Driven® Life*, p. 236

¹³Oh yes, you shaped me first inside, then out; you formed me in my mother's womb. ¹⁴I thank you, High God—you're breathtaking! Body and soul, I am marvelously made! I worship in adoration—what a creation! ¹⁵You know me inside and out, you know every bone in my body; you know exactly how I was made, bit by bit, how I was sculpted from nothing into something. ¹⁶Like an open book, you watched me grow from conception to birth; all the stages of my life were spread out before you, the days of my life all prepared before I'd even lived one day.

(Psalm 139:13–16 MSG)

Each of the five letters in the word S.H.A.P.E. represents a specific characteristic of your life:

- **S** _____ —"What am I gifted to do?"

- **H** _____ —"What passions do I have?"

- **A** _____ —"What do I naturally do better than others?"

- **P** _____ —"How has God wired me to navigate life?"

- **E** _____ —"Where have I been?" and "What have I learned?"

Determining a starting point gives you something to reflect on, to see how much God has helped you grow on your journey with him.

Only you can be you, and when you're not, the body of Christ suffers.

Signs of being *In S.H.A.P.E.*:

1. _____ in your mind

2. _____ in your heart

3. _____ in your life

Symptoms of being *Out of S.H.A.P.E.*:

1. _____ in your mind

2. _____ in your heart

3. _____ in your life

Whatever I have, wherever I am, I can make it through anything in the One who makes me who I am.

(Philippians 4:13 MSG)

Closing Thought: God wants you to live the abundant life—but you must do it through him. It's the key to discovering your Kingdom Purpose. God created you, and knows the unique masterpiece you are.

I'm grateful I made the commitment to identify my S.H.A.P.E. I was tired of not knowing who I was and what I was truly designed to do. You can do the same thing.

DISCUSSION QUESTIONS

1. Look back at the signs of being "In S.H.A.P.E." and the symptoms of being "Out of S.H.A.P.E." How do you see yourself right now? What hope, if any, are you feeling that this study will improve your S.H.A.P.E.? Share a thought with the group.

2. What is your reaction to being told you are God's masterpiece? How does this concept stand to impact your future with God? Do you feel like a masterpiece?

3. From our key verse, how does it make you feel to know you have a specific assignment from God to accomplish on earth, and that it is for his glory?

4. How would you define your life today? Would you be known as a Consumer (focused on getting), a Contributor (focused on giving), or a Cruiser (focused on getting by)? Share.

5. In what way do you think your group could ultimately benefit from your personal understanding of your S.H.A.P.E.?

LIVING ON PURPOSE

Fellowship

Membership in God's family is a great place to begin the S.H.A.P.E. discovery process. Through your interaction with other believers, you'll see more clearly how God wants to use your life for his service. At this initial stage of your S.H.A.P.E. journey, it's a good idea to identify someone you trust as a spiritual partner to help you fine-tune your discoveries. Choose a companion within your group, or find someone in your life who you believe will be a good sounding board. Then commit to meet with them regularly as you go through this material. In your first meeting with this partner, consider these questions:

1. Of the three things that tend to define people's lives, what would you say characterizes yours? Are you a trend-follower? A people-pleaser? Or do you seek first the heart of God?

2. What work do you think needs to be done in your life now to make sure you are, at the end of the day, fully identified with God?

PRAYER DIRECTION

Thank God for bringing you to this place where you are discovering who you are, who God has made you to be, and who you need to be in order to fulfill his specific design for you. Ask him to open your eyes and the eyes of your fellow group members, as you seek his purposes together, to reveal the specific contribution he created you for.

PUTTING IT INTO PRACTICE

As you begin your S.H.A.P.E. discovery journey, take time to identify the one thing you want God to do in you and through you over the next six weeks. What is that one thing you believe God wants you to fulfill for him? Write it here and in your S.H.A.P.E. Profile* on page 64.

*Each week, we'll ask you to transfer information from this section to your S.H.A.P.E. Profile, located in the back of this booklet following Session Six, on page 64.

Dear God:

Through this S.H.A.P.E. discovery series, I want you to

_____

_____

_____

Now commit this vision to God and expect to see results as you study this material.

With your spiritual partner and/or with your group's ministry champion, share what's on your heart as an initial road marker for your journey. Keep the destination in mind!

> . . . *The most important thing is that I complete my mission, the work that the Lord Jesus gave me* . . .

(Acts 20:24 NCV)

DIVING DEEPER

For maximum understanding of the material in this lesson, read chapter 1—"Masterpiece," from the book *S.H.A.P.E.: Finding and Fulfilling Your Unique Purpose for Life.*

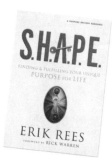

TWO

Unwrapping My Spiritual Gifts

God's Gifts Are the Key to Kingdom Purposes

CATCHING UP

- Tell the group what that *one thing* is you've identified as your goal for this study.

- Share a thought about what you learned in the first session.

- Talk about a gift you received that you considered perfect. What made it perfect in your eyes?

KEY VERSE

God has given gifts to each of you from his great variety of spiritual gifts. Manage them well so that God's generosity can flow through you.

1 Peter 4:10 (NLT)

Watch the Session Two video now and fill in the blanks in the outline in this guide. Refer back to the outline during your discussion time.

UNWRAPPING MY SPIRITUAL GIFTS

Now about spiritual gifts, brothers, I do not want you to be ignorant.

(1 Corinthians 12:1 NIV)

God's gifts are the key to the Kingdom Purpose he has set aside just for us.

In order to serve effectively, we need to understand the nature of spiritual gifts.

What spiritual gifts are *not*:

1. Your spiritual gifts are *not* your personality traits. (Your personality *can* provide a natural vehicle for expressing your gifts.)

2. Your spiritual gifts are *not* your natural talents.

3. Your spiritual gifts are *not* the same as the fruit of the Spirit (Galatians 5).

A spiritual gift *is:*

- A God-given _____

- _____ to every believer at conversion by the Holy Spirit

- To _____ God's love

- To _____ the body of Christ

God has given gifts to each of you from his great variety of spiritual gifts. Manage them well so that God's generosity can flow through you.

(1 Peter 4:10 NLT)

Why *does* God give spiritual gifts?

> *A spiritual gift is given to each of us as a means of helping the entire church.*
>
> (1 Corinthians 12:7 NLT)

Spiritual gifts are *not for* you or *about* you. They are for the specific purpose of
_____ the body of Christ—the church.

Every believer receives them.

> *. . . each of you has your own gift from God; one has this gift, another has that.*
>
> (1 Corinthians 7:7b TNIV)

God has given you a gift! If you're a believer, the Bible says you have the Spirit living in you, and gifts to use for his glory.

The key to discovering your gifts is two-fold:

1. Determine what gifts you think you may have.

2. Serve in various roles to see which ones bring the greatest fulfillment for you and the greatest results for God.

Allow Scripture to guide you to those gifts that are uniquely yours. Ask God to reveal how he wants you to use your gifts to accomplish his work in the world.

Many people discover their gifts as they minister to others. The more you serve, the more clearly you will see your gifts.

The ultimate goal is using your gifts to love and bless others.

> *[1]If I speak in the tongues of men and of angels, but have not love, I am only a resounding gong or a clanging cymbal. [2]If I have the gift of prophecy and can fathom all mysteries and all knowledge, and if I have a faith that can move mountains, but have not love, I am nothing. [3]If I give all I possess to the poor and surrender my body to the flames, but have not love, I gain nothing.*
>
> (1 Corinthians 13:1–3 NIV)

Are you serving to benefit others—or yourself?

Three common traps:

1. _____

God's Word says that all parts of the body are needed.

> *²¹The eye can never say to the hand, "I don't need you." The head can't say to the feet, "I don't need you." ²²In fact, some of the parts that seem weakest and least important are really the most necessary.*
>
> (1 Corinthians 12:21–22 NLT)

2. _____

Encourage everyone to be who God created them to be.

3. _____

Lack of position is not necessarily a lack of a gift.

Don't wait for God to fill in all the blanks before you start serving. Your group is a great place to begin!

> **Closing Thought:** The key is to serve in areas that best match your giftedness, and to start as soon as possible. When you do this you'll experience greater fulfillment and see greater fruitfulness for God. You were made by God to serve others.
>
> *We are better together.*

DISCUSSION QUESTIONS

1. While all spiritual gifts are given variously by God to be used for building up the body of Christ and for reaching the world with his message of hope, why do you think Paul tells us, in 1 Corinthians 13, that love is greater than these gifts? Explain.

2. Why is it important for us to learn to recognize our spiritual gifts? How is a spiritual gift different from a personality trait, a talent, or a characteristic? If you're not sure, this is a great opportunity to clarify your understanding with your group.

3. What can we do to avoid the traps Erik talked about: comparison, projection, and rejection? Which do you see yourself most easily falling into?

4. Do you already know your spiritual gifts? If so, share them with the group and how you've been using them in ministry.

5. Discuss how God might want to use your spiritual gifts to benefit the other members of your group. Is there a way you can serve one another?

LIVING ON PURPOSE

Ministry

The best way to discover your spiritual gifts is by serving the Body of Christ.

1. If you are not currently involved in serving, where do you think you could begin?

2. Take a few minutes to discuss ideas for serving your church or small group. How might these areas of service help you discover your spiritual gifts? Here are a few examples to start your conversation:

   • Providing child care during church services

   • Greeting worshipers as they arrive

   • Passing out information packets to new believers

   • Helping clean up after church services

   • Organizing teams of volunteers

   • Leading worship by singing or playing a musical instrument

   • Proofing, folding, or stuffing bulletins for weekend services

   • Taking meals to families in need

   • Driving people without transportation to church for worship services

   • Helping out part-time in the church office; doing whatever is needed

   • Think of others that might fit your area of giftedness—be creative!

PRAYER DIRECTION

Thank God for giving you spiritual gifts to unwrap over the course of this study. Ask him to reveal to each group member, individually, his or her unique area of giftedness through service to the body of Christ. Pray for one another to avoid and be kept from the traps of comparison, projection, and rejection.

S.H.A.P.E.

PUTTING IT INTO PRACTICE

As you read the list of spiritual gifts and their definitions below, think back on your own serving experiences. Then indicate "yes" if you feel you have the gift, "maybe" if you feel you might have the gift, or "no" if you think you don't have the gift. If you can, meet with your spiritual partner or your ministry champion this week to validate what you believe God is showing you.

Administration: The God-given special ability to serve and strengthen the body of Christ by effectively organizing resources and people in order to efficiently reach ministry goals. ❏ yes ❏ maybe ❏ no

Apostleship: The God-given special ability to serve and strengthen the body of Christ by launching and leading new ministry ventures that advance God's purposes and expand his kingdom. The original Greek meaning of the word is "sent one" (literally, one sent with authority, or as an ambassador). ❏ yes ❏ maybe ❏ no

Discernment: The God-given special ability to serve and strengthen the body of Christ by recognizing truth or error within a message, person, or event. ❏ yes ❏ maybe ❏ no

Encouragement: The God-given special ability to serve and strengthen the body of Christ by helping others live God-centered lives through inspiration, encouragement, counseling, and empowerment. ❏ yes ❏ maybe ❏ no

Evangelism: The God-given special ability to serve and strengthen the body of Christ by sharing the love of Christ with others in a way that draws them to respond by accepting God's free gift of eternal life. ❏ yes ❏ maybe ❏ no

Faith: The God-given special ability to serve and strengthen the body of Christ by stepping out in faith in order to see God's purposes accomplished, trusting him to handle any and all obstacles along the way. ❏ yes ❏ maybe ❏ no

Giving: The God-given special ability to serve and strengthen the body of Christ by joyfully supporting and funding various kingdom initiatives through material contributions beyond the tithe. ❏ yes ❏ maybe ❏ no

Healing: The God-given special ability to serve and strengthen the body of Christ by healing and restoring to health, beyond traditional and natural means, those who are sick, hurting, and suffering. ❏ yes ❏ maybe ❏ no

Helping: The God-given special ability to serve and strengthen the body of Christ by offering others assistance in reaching goals that glorify God and strengthen the body of Christ. This aptitude is sometimes referred to as the gift of "helps" or "service." ❏ yes ❏ maybe ❏ no

Hospitality: The God-given special ability to serve and strengthen the body of Christ by providing others with a warm and welcoming environment for fellowship. ❏ yes ❏ maybe ❏ no

Interpretation: The God-given special ability to serve and strengthen the body of Christ by understanding, at a specific time, God's message when spoken by another using a special language unknown to the others in attendance. ❏ yes ❏ maybe ❏ no

Knowledge: The God-given special ability to serve and strengthen the body of Christ by communicating God's truth to others in a way that promotes justice, honesty, and understanding. ❏ yes ❏ maybe ❏ no

Leadership: The God-given special ability to serve and strengthen the body of Christ by casting vision, stimulating spiritual growth, applying strategies, and achieving success where God's purposes are concerned. ❏ yes ❏ maybe ❏ no

Mercy: The God-given special ability to serve and strengthen the body of Christ by ministering to those who suffer physically, emotionally, spiritually, or relationally. Their actions are characterized by love, care, compassion, and kindness toward others. ❏ yes ❏ maybe ❏ no

Miracles: The God-given special ability to serve and strengthen the body of Christ through supernatural acts that bring validity to God and his power. ❏ yes ❏ maybe ❏ no

Pastoring: The God-given special ability to serve and strengthen the body of Christ by taking spiritual responsibility for a group of believers and equipping them to live Christ-centered lives. Shepherding is another word used for this particular gift. ❏ yes ❏ maybe ❏ no

Prophecy: The God-given special ability to serve and strengthen the body of Christ by offering messages from God that comfort, encourage, guide, warn, or reveal sin in a way that leads to repentance and spiritual growth. The original Greek meaning of this word is "to speak forth the truth." The gift of prophecy includes both "forth telling" (preaching), and "foretelling" (revelation). ❏ yes ❏ maybe ❏ no

Teaching: The God-given special ability to serve and strengthen the body of Christ by teaching sound doctrine in relevant ways, empowering people to gain a sound and mature spiritual education ❑ yes ❑ maybe ❑ no

Tongues: The God-given special ability to serve and strengthen the body of Christ by communicating God's message in a special language unknown to the speaker. ❑ yes ❑ maybe ❑ no

Wisdom: The God-given special ability to serve and strengthen the body of Christ by making wise decisions and counseling others with sound advice, all in accordance with God's will. ❑ yes ❑ maybe ❑ no

List the spiritual gifts you think you may have from the list above.

- _____
- _____
- _____
- _____
- _____

Think of a few ways you can start to use these gifts to serve others so you can clarify which ones you have.

Reminder: Be sure to transfer your personal list of gifts to your S.H.A.P.E. Profile on page 65.

DIVING DEEPER

More information about each gift is available in chapter 2—"Spiritual Gifts," from the book *S.H.A.P.E.: Finding and Fulfilling Your Unique Purpose for Life*.

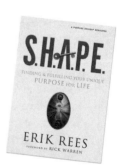

THREE

Hearing My Heartbeat

Discovering the God-given Desires of Your Heart

CATCHING UP

- What, if any, area of service did you discover or commit to this past week? Share the news with your group as an encouragement, or as a prayer request.

- From your study of the New Testament list of spiritual gifts in last week's Putting It into Practice section (page 16), share one new thing you learned about spiritual gifts.

- Talk about something exciting that happened in your life this past week. What made it exciting for you?

KEY VERSE

As a face is reflected in water, so the heart reflects the person.
Proverbs 27:19 (NLT)

Watch the Session Three video now and fill in the blanks in the outline in this guide. Refer back to the outline during your discussion time.

HEARING MY HEARTBEAT

Our emotional heartbeat is what we feel inside, when it races for some things and doesn't for others.

Delight yourself in the Lord and he will give you the desires of your heart.

(Psalm 37:4 NIV)

• What are the desires of your heart?

• How do you long to impact the lives of other people in this world?

We serve God by serving others.

[23]Whatever you do, work at it with all your heart, as working for the Lord, not for men, [24]since you know that you will receive an inheritance from the Lord as a reward. It is the Lord Christ you are serving.

(Colossians 3:23–24 NIV)

The ultimate contribution God has for you to make will align with the passions he has given you for his kingdom. Our hearts reflect our dreams and desires.

Key: Let God help you unlock your heart so it can start beating for him.

Ask yourself three questions:

1. Who do you love _____ ?

2. What needs do you love _____ ?

3. What challenges or causes do you love _____ ?

> I see countless thousands of souls that will one day spend eternity in hell if they do not find the Savior.
>
> —Dwight Moody, *Today in the Word*, February 1, 1997, pg. 6

Who Do You Love Serving?

God wants you to help him reach the people he has placed in your life.

1. Define your _____.

2. Determine which _____ you intend to meet in their lives.

What Needs Have God and Others Met in Your Own Life?

*He comforts us in all our troubles so that we can comfort others.
When others are troubled, we will be able to give them the same
comfort God has given us.*

(2 Corinthians 1:4 NLT)

God can use our weaknesses and failures as well as our strengths and passions as part of the masterpiece he is creating. Your suffering can help others get through their own suffering and discover their full potential.

What Needs Do You Love Meeting?

- _____ Needs: You love helping people discover Christ and reach their full potential in him.

- _____ Needs: You use your resources to help people with physical needs through practical expressions of love—food, clothing, shelter, and other simple necessities.

- _____ Needs: You enjoy helping people develop authentic, Christ-centered relationships with others, connecting people, helping them find and build satisfying relationships.

- _____ Needs: You find gratification helping people in pain go through their life situations with Christ, by counseling, encouraging, and listening to them.

- _____ Needs: You find special joy using your teaching gift to help others learn how to live life to its fullest.

- _____ Needs: You enjoy training, coaching, and consulting others to help them overcome barriers, reach their goals, and maximize their personal or professional potential.

What Causes Do You Love Conquering?

What eternal difference do you long to make for God? If you take time to listen, God will direct you to the cause he has personally chosen for you.

> **Closing Thought:** God has made each of us uniquely special. As a group, we need to affirm and help clarify his plans for each other.

DISCUSSION QUESTIONS

1. What kinds of things make your heart beat emotionally? Share with the group one or two chief desires of your heart.

2. Who do you think God wants you to reach? How can you identify your target audience?

3. Think about how God met you in difficult times in your life. How could you use those encounters to help someone else? How do you think God might use your gifts, abilities, personality, and experiences to reach your target audience? We'll consider this idea more during the coming week, but what is your initial response to these questions?

4. Our key verse for this week reminds us that everything we do, we do for God. He wants your heart to beat for him. What changes, if any, need to happen in your life in order for you to give God his heart's desire? Share with the group what God is revealing to you.

5. How could your God-given passions benefit your group? Discuss some ideas.

LIVING ON PURPOSE

Discipleship

It takes discipline to fine-tune our inner hearing so that we sense God's presence in our lives—and discipline is the deliberate choice that makes one a disciple.

1. Are there any activities you need to eliminate in order to help you hear God speak to your heart? Where can you adapt your schedule to make more time for listening to God?

2. How can you learn to recognize God's voice when you hear it, and how can this help you follow through on your own unique heartbeat for God? Consider Kay Warren's story. What do you think gave her the ability to hear God speak to her heart?

PRAYER DIRECTION

As you pray this week, start out as a group and then pair up for a more intimate time of conversation with God.

TOGETHER: Let God know how thankful you are for his inimitable mark on each life in the group. Ask him to reveal to each person in the room, as well as any group members who may be absent this week, their unique heartbeat for service.

IN PAIRS: Admit those things that might be keeping your heart from truly beating for God and for what he has given you to do. Ask God to take you deeper into what he is revealing. What might he want you to let go of in order to be more effective in service? What do you need to embrace?

PUTTING IT INTO PRACTICE

In order to help discover your heartbeat for ministry, take time this week to record your answers to the questions Erik offered as keys to unlocking your heart. Be ready to share some of the insights you gained in the next session:

1. Who do you love to serve?

   • Who am I most likely to profoundly influence for God?

   • What age range do I feel led to minister to?

   • What affinity group do I feel led to serve?

   • How could my particular gifts help them?

2. What needs do you love to meet?

   • What needs has God met in my life?

   • What category of need am I drawn to meet?
      ❑ Spiritual
      ❑ Physical
      ❑ Relational
      ❑ Emotional
      ❑ Educational
      ❑ Vocational

3. What causes do you love to conquer? Ask:

   • What cause or issue makes my heart race?

   • Where could I make the greatest impact for God?

   • If time or money weren't an issue, where would I donate my life?

Schedule time this week with your spiritual partner to talk about your answers and plan to report on at least one new finding at the next session. If greater clarity is needed on any point, consider touching base with your group's ministry champion.

Don't forget to transfer your answers from this section to your S.H.A.P.E. Profile on page 66.

What makes your heart beat?

❏ Abortion	❏ Divorce
❏ Homelessness	❏ Abuse/violence
❏ Drug abuse/recovery	❏ Law and/or justice system
❏ Alcoholism	❏ Educational issues
❏ Marriage/family issues	❏ At-risk children
❏ Environment	❏ Policy and/or politics
❏ Christ-centered parenting	❏ Ethics
❏ Poverty/hunger	❏ Compulsive behavior issues
❏ Financial stewardship	❏ Sanctity of life
❏ Deafness	❏ Health and/or fitness
❏ Sexuality and/or gender issues	❏ Disabilities and/or support
❏ HIV/AIDS	❏ Spiritual apathy
❏ Other	

DIVING DEEPER

For expanded understanding on any issues related to hearing your heartbeat, read chapter 3—"Heart," in the book, *S.H.A.P.E.: Finding and Fulfilling Your Ultimate Purpose for Life.*

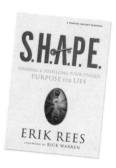

NOTES

FOUR

DISCOVERING MY NATURAL ABILITIES

CLARIFYING YOUR GOD-GIVEN STRENGTHS

CATCHING UP

- Did you consider the questions about your heartbeat for ministry from last week's Putting It into Practice section? Take a few moments to offer a new insight you gained.

- Here at the halfway point of this study, how is your perspective changing? Is God giving you a clearer picture of your unique life purpose? Share a thought or event with your group.

- Spend a minute or two sharing at least one thing for which you have a natural aptitude.

KEY VERSE:

"His master replied, 'Well done, good and faithful servant! You have been faithful with a few things; I will put you in charge of many things. Come and share your master's happiness!'"

Matthew 25:23 (NIV)

Watch the Session Four video now and fill in the blanks in the outline in this guide. Refer back to the outline during your discussion time.

DISCOVERING MY NATURAL ABILITIES

If we don't clearly identify our natural abilities, we can have a major problem down the road.

Natural abilities: a collection of strengths God wants us to use to fulfill our unique kingdom purpose in life.

All we need is to be available and aware.

God delights in willing _____.

The difference between an ordinary day and an extraordinary day is not so much what you do, but for whom you do it.

—Author Unknown

And whatever you do, whether in word or deed, do it all in the name of the Lord Jesus, giving thanks to God the Father through him.

(Colossians 3:17 NIV)

. . . the abilities you do have are a strong indication of what God wants you to do with your life. They are clues to knowing God's will for you . . . God doesn't waste abilities; he matches our calling and our capabilities.

—Rick Warren, *The Purpose Driven® Life*, p. 244

S.H.A.P.E.

Where do you naturally excel?

God is exceedingly qualified to put into action anything he has created. Remember: our _____ and _____ are there to show off his greatness and magnitude.

> *The LORD has given them special skills as jewelers, designers, weavers . . . They excel in all the crafts needed for the work.*

(Exodus 35:35 NLT)

God has also given you special _____ to excel in certain areas for him.

Reevaluate the abilities God has given you in light of his eternal purposes and the life situation in which he has placed you. It could open the door to a ministry more fulfilling than you ever imagined possible!

You'll find a list of fifty specialized abilities on page 38. The goal is for you to embrace the things you love to do, not just the things you can do.

One day each of us will have to give an account to God for what we did with the talents he gave us, so make the most of them now!

> *So then, each of us will give an account of himself to God.*

(Romans 14:12 NIV)

Parable of the Talents

Jesus told the story about a man who gave money to three of his servants before leaving on a journey. The first two put his money to work and gained a profit. But a third, fearing his master, buried the money. When the master returned, he rewarded the two who had increased his estate, praising them for being good and faithful. But the third wasn't as fortunate. His master shouted:

28 *"Take the talent from him and give it to the one who has the ten talents.* 29*For everyone who has will be given more, and he will have an abundance. Whoever does not have, even what he has will be taken from him."*

(Matthew 25:28–29 NIV)

Life is too short to settle for doing less than our _____ for God.

If we hold back the natural abilities God gave us at birth, or if we use those abilities for purposes that don't include God, they will not be used to their full capacity.

Closing Thought: Do you know the abilities you were born with? Do you know the things you love doing? Start figuring out ways to express those abilities in your everyday life. Grab hold of your natural abilities and aim them high for God's glory!

The greater danger for most of us is not that our aim is too high and we miss it, but that it is too low and we reach it.

—Michelangelo

DISCUSSION QUESTIONS

1. What characterizes an activity you love to do? Offer one or two top qualifications.

2. Talk about ways each of us can make deposits of love throughout a typical day, no matter what we are specializing in at the moment.

3. Think about the parable of the talents in Matthew 25:14–30. Why does it matter that we make the most of our abilities now? What could be the harm in putting them off or neglecting them?

4. Share with the group something you know you do well, but that you no longer do at all. Why did you stop doing it? Is there a way you could include it again in your lifestyle? Ask the group to pray for you to find that answer.

5. How could your natural abilities benefit your group? Share one way you think God could use something you know you do well.

LIVING ON PURPOSE

Ministry

One of the best places to discover both what we love to do and what we do well is through ministry. In many ways, ministry can be a better "school" than our college major or our job, because in ministry we are working selflessly, just for the sake of serving others.

1. How do you think ministry can help you?
    a) hear your heartbeat more distinctly, and
    b) develop your unique abilities?

2. If you are not involved in a life-changing ministry by now, explore some options this week. Recruit the help of your spiritual partner if needed in making this choice.

PRAYER DIRECTION

Thank God for the fact that he has given each of you natural talents and abilities. Ask God to help you see more clearly how he wants you to use them. If you're already using them, ask him what more he has for you. Don't miss God's best for your life!

PUTTING IT INTO PRACTICE

Set aside time this week to consider those things you naturally do well.

Use the list on pages 39 and 40 to help you recognize what God has gifted you to do. After you mark it, pick the top five you most excel at and love doing.

Love It!—You can't imagine life without these activities. They make your day complete. Given a choice, you would do these things full-time. These abilities are the way you will meet the needs of the people group you identified in the last chapter. They can be—but don't have to be—part of your job. Your nine-to-five life may be just tent-making, as it was for the apostle Paul. If you are unsatisfied by what you do full-time, finding what you love to do most could become what you do full-time.

Like It!—You may enjoy these abilities/activities, but don't need to do them on a regular basis in order to feel satisfied. Your attitude toward them is "I can take it or leave it." For example, you may enjoy coaching or teaching, but these things don't satisfy you like the things you really love.

Live Without!—These abilities/activities leave you feeling slightly deflated and disappointed, compared to what you love doing. When faced with the prospect of having to do these things, your immediate response is to think about not doing them. When you have to carry out these responsibilities on a frequent basis, you feel drained. You may be able to adequately perform these tasks, but you have little or no desire to do them.

Fifty Specialized Abilities			
ABILITY	**LOVE IT**	**LIKE IT**	**COULD LIVE WITHOUT IT**
1. Adapting: The ability to adjust, change, alter, modify			
2. Administering: The ability to govern, run, rule			
3. Analyzing: The ability to examine, investigate, probe, evaluate			
4. Building: The ability to construct, make, assemble			
5. Coaching: The ability to prepare, instruct, train, equip, develop			
6. Communicating: The ability to share, convey, impart			
7. Computing: The ability to add, estimate, total, calculate			
8. Connecting: The ability to link, involve, relate			
9. Consulting: The ability to advise, discuss, confer			
10. Cooking: The ability to prepare, serve, feed, or cater			
11. Coordinating: The ability to organize, match, harmonize			
12. Counseling: The ability to guide, advise, support, listen, or care for			
13. Competing: The ability to contend, win, battle			
14. Decorating: The ability to beautify, enhance, adorn			
15. Designing: The ability to draw, create, picture, outline			
16. Developing: The ability to expand, grow, advance, increase			
17. Directing: The ability to aim, oversee, manage, supervise			
18. Editing: The ability to correct, amend, alter, improve			
19. Encouraging: The ability to cheer, inspire, support			
20. Engineering: The ability to construct, design, plan			
21. Facilitating: The ability to help, aid, assist, make possible			
22. Forecasting: The ability to predict, calculate, see trends, patterns, and themes			
23. Implementing: The ability to apply, execute, make happen			
24. Improving: The ability to better, enhance, further, enrich			
25. Influencing: The ability to effect, sway, shape, change			
26. Landscaping: The ability to garden, plant, improve			

Continued on page 40

27. Leading: The ability to pave the way, direct, excel, win
28. Learning: The ability to study, gather, understand, improve, expand self
29. Managing: The ability to run, handle, oversee
30. Mentoring: The ability to advise, guide, teach
31. Motivating: The ability to provoke, induce, prompt
32. Negotiating: The ability to discuss, consult, settle
33. Operating: The ability to run mechanical or technical things
34. Organizing: The ability to simplify, arrange, fix, classify, coordinate
35. Performing: The ability to sing, speak, play an instrument, act out
36. Pioneering: The ability to bring about something new, ground-breaking, original
37. Planning: The ability to arrange, map out, prepare
38. Promoting: The ability to sell, sponsor, endorse, showcase
39. Recruiting: The ability to draft, enlist, hire, engage
40. Repairing: The ability to fix, mend, restore, heal
41. Researching: The ability to seek, gather, examine, study
42. Resourcing: The ability to furnish, provide, deliver
43. Serving: The ability to help, assist, fulfill
44. Strategizing: The ability to think ahead, calculate, scheme
45. Teaching: The ability to explain, demonstrate, tutor
46. Translating: The ability to interpret, decode, explain, speak
47. Traveling: The ability to journey, visit, explore
48. Visualizing: The ability to picture, imagine, envision, dream, conceptualize
49. Welcoming: The ability to entertain, greet, embrace, make comfortable
50. Writing: The ability to compose, create, record

List below your top five natural abilities.

1. _____

2. _____

3. _____

4. _____

5. _____

(Be sure you transfer these to your S.H.A.P.E. Profile on page 67.)

How can you use these abilities to serve others this next week?

As you complete this list, note whether or not you are currently using that ability and if so, where.

Now review the list and ask yourself, "Where have I lost focus?", "Where do I need to sharpen my focus?" or "Where do I think God wants to stretch me?"

For added insight, share this list with your spiritual partner or with your group's ministry champion.

Now have a brainstorming session with God. How might he want to use the talents and abilities he has given you? Write down what he is revealing to you.

DIVING DEEPER

Explore your natural abilities in greater depth by reading chapter 4—"Abilities," in the book *S.H.A.P.E.: Finding and Fulfilling Your Unique Purpose for Life.*

FIVE

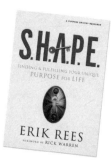

RECOGNIZING MY PERSONALITY

GOD LOVES VARIETY

CATCHING UP

- What did you learn through the review of your natural abilities? Did the additional list help you recognize more possibilities? Share one new insight with the group.

- Were you able to meet with your spiritual partner? How did that connection help expand or affirm what God is showing you?

- Now that you've been together a few weeks, take a few minutes to go around the room and affirm in each person something that has blessed the group.

KEY VERSE

God works through different people in different ways, but it is the same God who achieves his purpose through them all.

1 Corinthians 12:6 (PH)

Watch the Session Five video now and fill in the blanks in the outline in this guide. Refer back to the outline during your discussion time

RECOGNIZING MY PERSONALITY

God loves variety. There is no "wrong" or "right" temperament. God wants to use them all. God doesn't measure people the way most of us do.

"The Lord does not look at the things man looks at. Man looks at the outward appearance, but the Lord looks at the heart."

(1 Samuel 16:7b NIV)

The world places value on externals like prestige, position, and wealth; God places the highest value on less visible aspects of our lives.

The personality you have is God's _____ to you. He created it and gave it to you to use for his glory.

> Personality: The complex of characteristics that distinguishes an individual.
>
> —Webster's Dictionary

Your personality takes center stage in all areas of your life!

Ideas about Personality Traits

Indisputable truth: God has instilled a _____ in each one of us.

Two broad areas:

- How you _____ to others
- How you _____ to opportunities

Your Kingdom Purpose is all about people, so it is important to discover how you relate to those around you. Because you'll encounter many serving opportunities throughout your life, understanding how you react to various situations helps you make the best choices.

How I Relate to Others

_____ or _____

_____ or _____

_____ or _____

How I Respond to Opportunities

_____ or _____

_____ or _____

_____ or _____

_____ or _____

_____ or _____

Give yourself permission to be who God made you to be!

Closing Thought: The key is to determine how you best relate to others and respond to serving opportunities. Think of a few ways to start expressing your personality in ministry this next week.

DISCUSSION QUESTIONS

1. How do you think discovering the way God has wired your unique personality will help you fulfill your Kingdom Purpose?

2. Erik asked: "If you had the opportunity to choose the ideal situation that would enable you to make the greatest difference for God, what would it look like?" Respond to that question by thinking back over recent life opportunities. Which brought the greatest sense of fulfillment and purpose?

3. Why do we tend to think of certain personality traits as "wrong" or "right"? How have you seen your personality up to now? Had it occurred to you before this lesson that God has a divine use for your personality—that he intentionally made you the way you are? Share one or two key thoughts with the group.

4. What difference does it make for you to know that God intentionally made you the way you are, whether you are outgoing or reserved, self-expressive or self-controlled, cooperative or competitive? Others may see one trait as preferred, but God made all traits specifically for his deliberate use.

5. How can our personalities bless others in our small group? Take a moment or two to affirm a characteristic in each group member.

LIVING ON PURPOSE

Worship

> A life of purpose is how we live, while the purpose of worship is one of the reasons why we live . . . The soil of a worshiping heart is that which allows the seed of faith to grow and produce fruit. Rick Warren has taught me, "Surrender is not the best way to live; it is the only way to live." So we make it our goal to please God.
>
> —Rick Muchow, *The Worship Answer Book*, pp.119, 122

More than any other quality, our personalities are a reflection of God. He has created us in his image. None of us is exactly like God, but each of us is like God in some way.

1. What role does your personality play in the way you express worship to God?

2. In addition to serving in ministry, what other ways might God want to use your specific personality traits? How is the full surrender of your personality for his use an expression of worship to God? Share with the group a memory of a time God used you, simply because you're—you! How was God glorified through this example?

3. How is our cooperation with God in allowing his Spirit to infuse and use us as he made us an act of worship? Think about steps you can take to make sure you are worshiping God in this way on a regular basis.

PRAYER DIRECTION

Thank God for the personalities he has given each of you. Ask him to help you see where a trait needs to be submitted to the power of his Spirit for change and ask him to show you how to be yourself for his sake. Ask for the power that only comes through a surrendered life of worship.

PUTTING IT INTO PRACTICE

Take time this week to evaluate your personality tendencies based on the questions Erik posed during this session. If possible, review your findings with your spiritual partner, or with someone who knows you well, for added insight. Determine how you will use your unique personality traits in ministry. And remember: no answer is right or wrong, better or worse. We're all distinct, just as God made us! And we are made for his purpose.

How I Relate to Others

Circle the words below that BEST describe how you relate to others. You can circle the "X" in the middle if your personality tends to include both traits:

Outgoing ——————————— X ——————————— Reserved

Self-expressive ——————————— X ——————————— Self-controlled

Cooperative ——————————— X ——————————— Competitive

How I Respond to Opportunities

Circle the words below that BEST describe how you respond to serving opportunities. You can circle the "X" in the middle if you tend to embrace opportunities that include both traits:

High Risk ——————————— X ——————————— Low Risk

People Driven ——————————— X ——————————— Project Driven

Follow ——————————— X ——————————— Lead

Team ——————————— X ——————————— Solo

Routine ——————————— X ——————————— Variety

Now transfer your results to your S.H.A.P.E. Profile on page 68.

DIVING DEEPER

Learn more about your natural abilities in chapter 5—
"Personality," from the book *S.H.A.P.E.: Finding and
Fulfilling Your Unique Purpose for Life.*

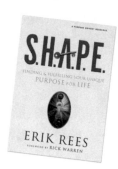

SIX

UNDERSTANDING
MY EXPERIENCES

GOD USES OUR EXPERIENCES
FOR HIS GLORY

S.H.A.P.E.

CATCHING UP

- What did you learn through the review of your personality tendencies? Did the additional list help you recognize more possibilities? If possible, share one new insight with the group.

- Tell the group one new lesson you've learned about your God-given personality, or share a story about how God has used you already to impact others' lives.

- As you head in to this last session, briefly share what this series has meant to you so far and how you think it will impact your future.

KEY VERSE

Praise be to the God and Father of our Lord Jesus Christ, the Father of compassion and the God of all comfort, who comforts us in all our troubles, so that we can comfort those in any trouble with the comfort we ourselves have received from God.

2 Corinthians 1:3–4 (NIV)

Watch the Session Six video now and fill in the blanks in the outline in this guide. Refer back to the outline during your discussion time.

UNDERSTANDING MY EXPERIENCES

There is purpose in your _____.

> *And we know that God causes everything to work together for the good of those who love God and are called according to his purpose for them.*
>
> (Romans 8:28 NLT)

God desires to take all of our experiences—the good and the bad—and use them for his glory.

JOSEPH Genesis 37–50

- Betrayed by his brothers
- Sold into slavery
- Thrown into prison

- Rose to become the second most powerful man in Egypt
- Saved the lives of millions
- Never forgot that God was in control

> *You intended to harm me, but God intended it for good to accomplish what is now being done, the saving of many lives.*
>
> (Genesis 50:20 NIV)

As God lovingly crafts the masterpiece of our lives, he uses every _____ to complete the finished product.

Consider the events of your life that have helped S.H.A.P.E. the person you are today:

- Childhood joys and sorrows
- The pain and thrill of adolescence
- The struggle and accomplishment of adulthood

THE GALLERY OF YOUR LIFE

The possibilities are almost limitless for your life achievements and experiences to become action steps for God.

God's delight and pride in you is not based on what is celebrated by the world.

Think of your experiences in these five general areas:

Positive Portrait

1. _____ — An award

2. _____ — A pattern of achievement

3. _____ — A godly marriage or a friendship that comforts or challenges you

4. _____ — Academic degrees or training certificates, or ongoing development in areas of special interest

5. _____ — A history of success in sharing your faith or leading Christians to deeper insight; your own acceptance of Christ and spiritual growth

Painful Portrait

God wants to use your painful experiences to minister to others as well . . . times when your pain threshold was tested and your endurance was stretched to the breaking point.

- Divorce

- Abuse

- Death

- Alcoholism

- Cancer

- Depression

- Job loss

- Bankruptcy

- Eating disorders

- Miscarriages

- Suicide

- Abortion

- Affairs

Think about the good that can come from your suffering. How can your crisis become a catalyst for Christ?

Take a Test-Drive

Challenge everyone in your group to commit to taking a ninety-day
_____. It's during this trip you will start to define your
S.H.A.P.E. and begin to refine your Kingdom Purpose.

Experiment with various ministry opportunities. Start slow and start small,
but make sure you START! Don't wait for perfect conditions—God blesses a
moving target.

Four great places to use your S.H.A.P.E. and start serving during your test-drive:

1. Use your S.H.A.P.E. to make deposits of love in your _____ .

2. Use your S.H.A.P.E. to serve others at _____ .

3. Use your S.H.A.P.E. to volunteer at your _____ .

4. Express your S.H.A.P.E. within your _____ group.

You now have the opportunity to continue what God has started as you run the
next leg of your race with him. Live faithful to God and finish fulfilled by him.

Closing Thought: Why not explore serving together as a group?
Discover how amazingly God will use your various gifts when your
group becomes your team.

The Final Goal:

_"Well done, good and faithful servant! You have been faithful with a few
things; I will put you in charge of many things. Come and share your
master's happiness!"_

(Matthew 25:21 NIV)

Discussion Questions

1. Share with your group where you will start your ninety-day test-drive—at home, work, church, or in your small group. Explain.

2. Share with your group a few positive portraits from your past and how they could provide a platform to serve others.

3. Discuss how your salvation experience could be a springboard for ministry. How might God want to use your testimony to reach others?

4. Share a few of your painful portraits along with your thoughts on how they could become a catalyst for Christ. Think about who, in particular, these events might help you reach, either in ministry or evangelism.

5. Share a few ideas about how your experiences can benefit others in your group.

6. How do you think you will know when you are exactly where God wants you?

7. SERIES FINAL: What have you learned as a result of this series that has helped settle any questions about God's purpose in your life? What do you plan to do as a result of these lessons?

Let your next group gathering be a celebration of S.H.A.P.E. Use that time to share additional insights God has given you as a result of this series and to share your S.H.A.P.E. Profiles.

LIVING ON PURPOSE

Evangelism

No matter how painful your past, God can use that pain as a catalyst for loving others.

1. Plan to take time for a longer visit to God's art gallery soon, and perhaps on a semi-annual basis as a means of life review.

   • Carefully study what God shows you.

   • Record in a notebook what he is revealing to you, what he taught you, and how you think he can use this lesson for the future.

   • Use this time for focused conversation with God, asking him to reveal his heart to you.

   • Ask him for breakthrough vision, and then plan to use what he shows you to reach others for Christ with your life.

2. Determine in your heart to have a personal retreat with God at least once a year to review your S.H.A.P.E., and then meet with your group or your spiritual partner to assess how effectively it is being used in reaching the lost for Christ.

3. Think back on Dwight Moody's example, of seeing others as "thousands of souls that will one day spend eternity in hell if they do not find the Savior." Recognize that the overriding purpose of your S.H.A.P.E. is to serve God by serving others.

PRAYER DIRECTION

Thank God for this series, and for showing you the many reasons he has for making each of you exactly who you are. Pray around the room for one another's needs, asking God to reveal to you through whatever circumstance you are experiencing right now a way he can use it for service, either now or in the future. Acknowledge it as part of your S.H.A.P.E.

PUTTING IT INTO PRACTICE

What are some of the portraits from the gallery of your life that you feel God can use?

Three Positive Portraits:

- _____
  _____
  _____
  _____

- _____
  _____
  _____
  _____

- _____
  _____
  _____
  _____

S.H.A.P.E.

Three Painful Portraits:

* _____

  _____

  _____

  _____

* _____

  _____

  _____

  _____

* _____

  _____

  _____

  _____

Be sure to complete your S.H.A.P.E. Profile by transferring these answers over to page 69.

Whatever you do before you complete this series, make sure that you've begun to put some of its steps into practice in your life. You are God's masterpiece, but just like those popular makeover shows, the new look is only temporary if you don't continue to apply its lessons daily. Where have you begun to use your S.H.A.P.E. on a regular basis? Remember: *God blesses a moving target!*

This week, and from now on, be sure you are using your S.H.A.P.E. in these four life arenas:

1. In your home, through regular deposits of love
2. In the workplace, by serving others
3. At church as a volunteer
4. In your small group as God determines the need

May God clarify, simplify, and illuminate the purpose for which he has uniquely S.H.A.P.E.d you as you walk with him every day of your life. Let the journey begin!

DIVING DEEPER

Expand your understanding regarding the value of your past experiences by reading chapter 6—"Experiences," in the book *S.H.A.P.E.: Finding and Fulfilling Your Unique Purpose for Life.*

MY S.H.A.P.E. PROFILE

THE ONE THING:

Dear God:

Through this S.H.A.P.E. discovery series, I want you to _____

_____

_____

_____

_____

_____

_____

_____

_____

_____

_____

_____

_____

_____

_____

SPIRITUAL GIFTS: WHAT I'M GIFTED TO DO

• The spiritual gifts I believe God has given me are:

• I feel I could use these gifts in the following ways to serve others:

HEART: WHAT I HAVE A PASSION FOR

- Whom I love to serve:

- The needs I love to meet in another person's life:

- The cause I feel God wants me to help conquer for him:

ABILITIES: WHERE I NATURALLY EXCEL

- My top abilities are:

PERSONALITY: HOW GOD HAS WIRED ME

I tend to relate to others by being:

Outgoing _____ X _____ Reserved

Self-expressive _____ X _____ Self-controlled

Cooperative _____ X _____ Competitive

I tend to respond to opportunities that are:

High Risk _____ X _____ Low Risk

People Driven _____ X _____ Project Driven

Follow _____ X _____ Lead

Team _____ X _____ Solo

Routine _____ X _____ Variety

EXPERIENCES: WHERE I HAVE BEEN

- My positive experiences include:

- Areas in which I feel I could help another person include:

- My painful experiences include:

- These are areas God has helped me through that I feel I could help another person through:

Conclusion: Based on my S.H.A.P.E. Profile, I think I should explore the following ideas for ministry:

-
-
-
-

GROUP
RESOURCES

HELPS FOR HOSTS

TOP TEN IDEAS FOR NEW HOSTS

Congratulations! As the host of your small group, you have responded to the call to help shepherd Jesus' flock. Few other tasks in the family of God surpass the contribution you will be making. As you prepare to facilitate your group, whether it is one session or the entire series, here are a few thoughts to keep in mind.

Remember you are not alone. God knows everything about you, and he knew you would be asked to facilitate your group. Even though you may not feel ready, this is common for all good hosts. God promises, *"I will never leave you; I will never abandon you"* (Hebrews 13:5 TEV). Whether you are facilitating for one evening, several weeks, or a lifetime, you will be blessed as you serve.

1. **Don't try to do it alone.** Pray right now for God to help you build a healthy team. If you can enlist a co-host to help you shepherd the group, you will find your experience much richer. This is your chance to involve as many people as you can in building a healthy group. All you have to do is ask people to help. You'll be surprised at the response.

2. **Be friendly and be yourself.** God wants to use your unique gifts and temperament. Be sure to greet people at the door with a big smile . . . this can set the mood for the whole gathering. Remember, they are taking as big a step as you are to show up at your house! Don't try to do things exactly like another host; do them in a way that fits you. Admit when you don't have an answer and apologize when you make a mistake. Your group will love you for it and you'll sleep better at night.

3. **Prepare for your meeting ahead of time.** Review the session and write down your responses to each question. Pay special attention to exercises that ask group members to do something other than engage in discussion. These exercises will help your group live what the Bible teaches, not just talk about it. Be sure you understand how an exercise works. If the exercise employs one of the items in the Group Resources section (such as the Purpose Driven Group Guidelines), be sure to look over that item so you'll know how it works.

4. **Pray for your group members by name.** Before you begin your session, take a few moments and pray for each member by name. You may want to review the prayer list at least once a week. Ask God to use your time together to touch the heart of every person in your group. Expect God to lead you to whomever he wants you to encourage or challenge in a special way. If you listen, God will surely lead.

5. **When you ask a question, be patient.** Someone will eventually respond. Sometimes people need a moment or two of silence to think about the question. If silence doesn't bother you, it won't bother anyone else. After someone responds, affirm the response with a simple "thanks" or "great answer." Then ask, "How about somebody else?" or "Would someone who hasn't shared like to add anything?" Be sensitive to new people or reluctant members who aren't ready to say, pray, or do anything. If you give them a safe setting, they will blossom over time. If someone in your group is a "wall flower" who sits silently through every session, consider talking to them privately and encouraging them to participate. Let them know how important they are to you—that they are loved and appreciated, and that the group would value their input. Remember, still water often runs deep.

6. **Provide transitions between questions.** Ask if anyone would like to read the paragraph or Bible passage. Don't call on anyone, but ask for a volunteer, and then be patient until someone begins. Be sure to thank the person who reads aloud.

7. **Break into smaller groups occasionally.** With a greater opportunity to talk in a small circle, people will connect more with the study, apply more quickly what they're learning, and ultimately get more out of their small group experience. A small circle also encourages a quiet person to participate and tends to minimize the effects of a more vocal or dominant member.

8. **Small circles are also helpful during prayer time.** People who are unaccustomed to praying aloud will feel more comfortable trying it with just two or three others. Also, prayer requests won't take as much time, so circles will have more time to actually pray. When you gather back with the whole group, you can have one person from each circle briefly update everyone on the prayer requests from their subgroups. The other great aspect of subgrouping is that it fosters leadership development. As you ask people in the group to facilitate discussion or to lead a prayer circle, it gives them a small leadership step that can build their confidence.

9. **Rotate facilitators occasionally.** You may be perfectly capable of hosting each time, but you will help others grow in their faith and gifts if you give them opportunities to host the group.

10. **One final challenge (for new or first-time hosts).** Before your first opportunity to lead, look up each of the five passages listed below. Read each one as a devotional exercise to help prepare you with a shepherd's heart. Trust us on this one. If you do this, you will be more than ready for your first meeting.

Matthew 9:36–38 (NIV)

[36] When Jesus saw the crowds, he had compassion on them, because they were harassed and helpless, like sheep without a shepherd. [37] Then he said to his disciples, "The harvest is plentiful but the workers are few. [38] Ask the Lord of the harvest, therefore, to send out workers into his harvest field."

John 10:14–15 (NIV)

[14] I am the good shepherd; I know my sheep and my sheep know me—[15] just as the Father knows me and I know the Father—and I lay down my life for the sheep.

1 Peter 5:2–4 (NIV)

[2] Be shepherds of God's flock that is under your care, serving as overseers—not because you must, but because you are willing, as God wants you to be; [3] not greedy for money, but eager to serve; not lording it over those entrusted to you, but being examples to the flock. [4] And when the Chief Shepherd appears, you will receive the crown of glory that will never fade away.

Philippians 2:1–5 (NIV)

[1] If you have any encouragement from being united with Christ, if any comfort from his love, if any fellowship with the Spirit, if any tenderness and compassion, [2] then make my joy complete by being like-minded, having the same love, being one in spirit and purpose. [3] Do nothing out of selfish ambition or vain conceit, but in humility consider others better than yourselves. [4] Each of you should look not only to your own interests, but also to the interests of others. [5] Your attitude should be the same as that of Jesus Christ.

Hebrews 10:23–25 (NIV)

^{23}Let us hold unswervingly to the hope we profess, for he who promised is faithful. ^{24}And let us consider how we may spur one another on toward love and good deeds. ^{25}Let us not give up meeting together, as some are in the habit of doing, but let us encourage one another—and all the more as you see the Day approaching.

1 Thessalonians 2:7–8, 11–12 (NIV)

^{7}. . . but we were gentle among you, like a mother caring for her little children. 8We loved you so much that we were delighted to share with you not only the Gospel of God but our lives as well, because you had become so dear to us. . . . ^{11}For you know that we dealt with each of you as a father deals with his own children, ^{12}encouraging, comforting and urging you to live lives worthy of God, who calls you into his kingdom and glory.

FREQUENTLY ASKED QUESTIONS

How long will this group meet?

S.H.A.P.E.: Finding and Fulfilling Your Unique Purpose for Life is six sessions long. We encourage your group to add a seventh session for a celebration. In your final session, each group member may decide if he or she desires to continue on for another study. At that time you may also want to do some informal evaluation, discuss your group guidelines, and decide which study you want to do next. We recommend you visit our website at *www.purposedriven.com* for more video-based small group studies.

Who is the host?

The host is the person who coordinates and facilitates your group meetings. In addition to a host, we encourage you to select one or more group members to lead your group discussions. Several other responsibilities can be rotated, including refreshments, prayer requests, worship, or keeping up with those who miss a meeting. Shared ownership in the group helps everybody grow.

Where do we find new group members?

Recruiting new members can be a challenge for groups, especially new groups with just a few people, or existing groups that lose a few people along the way. We encourage you to use the Circles of Life diagram on page 80 of this workbook to brainstorm a list of people from your workplace, church, school, neighborhood, family, and so on. Then pray for the people on each member's list. Allow each member to invite several people from their list. Some groups fear that newcomers will interrupt the intimacy that members have built over time. However, groups that welcome newcomers generally gain strength with the infusion of new blood. Remember, the next person you add just might become a friend for eternity. Logistically, groups find different ways to add members. Some groups remain permanently open, while others choose to open periodically, such as at the beginning or end of a study. If your group becomes too large for easy, face-to-face conversations, you can subgroup, forming a second discussion group in another room.

How do we handle the childcare needs in our group?

Childcare needs must be handled very carefully. This is a sensitive issue. We suggest you seek creative solutions as a group. One common solution is to have the adults meet in the living room and share the cost of a baby sitter (or two) who can be with the kids in another part of the house. Another popular option is to have one home for the kids and a second home (close by) for the adults. If desired, the adults could rotate the responsibility of providing a lesson for the kids. This last option is great with school age kids and can be a huge blessing to families.

Purpose Driven Group Guidelines

It's a good idea for every group to put words to their shared values, expectations, and commitments. Such guidelines will help you avoid unspoken agendas and unmet expectations. We recommend you discuss your guidelines during Session One in order to lay the foundation for a healthy group experience. Feel free to modify anything that does not work for your group.

We agree to the following values:

Clear Purpose	To grow healthy spiritual lives by building a healthy small group community
Group Attendance	To give priority to the group meeting (call if I am absent or late)
Safe Environment	To create a safe place where people can be heard and feel loved (no quick answers, snap judgments, or simple fixes)
Be Confidential	To keep anything that is shared strictly confidential and within the group
Conflict Resolution	To avoid gossip and to immediately resolve any concerns by following the principles of Matthew 18:15–17
Spiritual Health	To give group members permission to speak into my life and help me live a healthy, balanced spiritual life that is pleasing to God
Limit Our Freedom	To limit our freedom by not serving or consuming alcohol during small group meetings or events so as to avoid causing a weaker brother or sister to stumble (1 Corinthians 8:1–13; Romans 14:19–21)
Welcome Newcomers	To invite friends who might benefit from this study and warmly welcome newcomers
Building Relationships	To get to know the other members of the group and pray for them regularly
Other	_____
	_____
	_____

We have also discussed and agree on the following items:

Child Care

_____

_____

Starting Time

_____

Ending Time

_____

If you haven't already done so, take a few minutes to fill out the Small Group Calendar on page 84.

CIRCLES OF LIFE: SMALL GROUP CONNECTIONS

Discover who you can connect in community

Use this chart to help carry out one of the values in the Purpose Driven Group Guidelines, to "Welcome Newcomers."

"Follow me, and I will make you fishers of men." (Matthew 4:19 KJV)

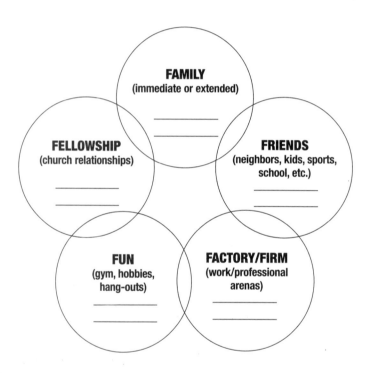

Follow this simple three-step process:

1. List one to two people in each circle.

2. Prayerfully select one person or couple from your list and tell your group about them.

3. Give them a call and invite them to your next meeting. Over fifty percent of those invited to a small group say, "Yes!"

SMALL GROUP PRAYER AND PRAISE REPORT

This is a place where you can write each other's requests for prayer. You can also make a note when God answers a prayer. Pray for each other's requests. If you're new to group prayer, it's okay to pray silently or to pray by using just one sentence: "God, please help _____ to _____ ."

DATE	PERSON	PRAYER REQUEST	PRAISE REPORT

SMALL GROUP PRAYER AND PRAISE REPORT

DATE	PERSON	PRAYER REQUEST	PRAISE REPORT

Small Group Prayer and Praise Report

DATE	PERSON	PRAYER REQUEST	PRAISE REPORT

SMALL GROUP CALENDAR

Healthy groups share responsibilities and group ownership. It might take some time for this to develop. Shared ownership ensures that responsibility for the group doesn't fall to one person. Use the calendar to keep track of social events, mission projects, birthdays, or days off. Complete this calendar at your first or second meeting. Planning ahead will increase attendance and shared ownership.

DATE	LESSON	LOCATION	FACILITATOR	SNACK OR MEAL
10/22	Session 2	Steve and Laura	Bill Jones	John and Alice

ANSWER KEY

SESSION ONE: ONLY YOU CAN BE YOU

"What will be the **contribution** of my life?"

Your specific contribution to the body of Christ, within your generation, that causes you to totally **depend** on God and authentically **display** his love toward others—all through the expression of your uniqueness.

1. **Trends**

2. What others **tell** them

3. God's **truth**

Spiritual Gifts—"What am I gifted to do?"
Heart—"What passions do I have?"
Abilities—"What do I naturally do better than others?"
Personality—"How has God wired me to navigate life?"
Experiences—"Where have I been?" and "What have I learned?"

1. **Focus** in your mind
2. **Fulfillment** in your heart
3. **Fruitfulness** in your life

1. **Frustration** in your mind
2. **Fatigue** in your heart
3. **Fear** in your life

SESSION TWO: UNWRAPPING MY SPIRITUAL GIFTS

- A God-given **special ability**
- **Given** to every believer at conversion by the Holy Spirit
- To **share** God's love
- To **strengthen** the body of Christ

Spiritual gifts . . . are for the specific purpose of **blessing** the body of Christ—the church.

1. **Comparison**
2. **Projection**
3. **Rejection**

SESSION THREE: HEARING MY HEARTBEAT

1. Who do you love **serving**?
2. What needs do you love **meeting**?
3. What challenges or causes do you love **conquering**?

1. Define your **target**.
2. Determine which **needs** you intend to meet in their lives.

- **Spiritual** Needs
- **Physical** Needs
- **Relational** Needs
- **Emotional** Needs
- **Educational** Needs
- **Vocational** Needs

SESSION FOUR: DISCOVERING MY NATURAL ABILITIES

God delights in willing **hearts**.

God is exceedingly qualified to put into action anything he has created. Remember: our **strengths** and **abilities** are there to show off his greatness and magnitude.

God has also given you special **abilities** to excel in certain areas for him. Life is too short to settle for doing less than our **best** for God.

SESSION FIVE: RECOGNIZING MY PERSONALITY

The personality you have is God's **gift** to you. He created it and gave it to you to use for his glory.

God has instilled a **unique personality** in each one of us.

- How you **relate** to others
- How you **respond** to opportunities

How I Relate To Others

Outgoing _____ or _____ **Reserved**
Self-expressive _____ or _____ **Self-controlled**
Cooperative _____ or _____ **Competitive**

How I Relate To Opportunities

High Risk _____ or _____ **Low Risk**
People Driven _____ or _____ **Project Driven**
Follow _____ or _____ **Lead**
Team _____ or _____ **Solo**
Routine _____ or _____ **Variety**

Session Six: Understanding My Experiences

There is purpose in your **past.**
As God lovingly crafts the masterpiece of our lives, he uses every **experience** to complete the finished product.

1. **Personally**—An award
2. **Vocationally**—A pattern of achievement
3. **Relationally**—A godly marriage or a friendship that comforts or challenges you.
4. **Educationally**—Academic degrees or training certificates, or ongoing development in areas of special interest
5. **Spiritually**—A history of success in sharing your faith or leading Christians to deeper insight; your own acceptance of Christ and spiritual growth

Challenge everyone in your group to commit to taking a ninety-day **test-drive**.

1. Use your S.H.A.P.E. to make deposits of love in your **home**.
2. Use your S.H.A.P.E. to serve others at **work**.
3. Use your S.H.A.P.E. to volunteer at your **church**.
4. Express your S.H.A.P.E. within your **small** group.

KEY VERSES

One of the most effective ways to drive deeply into our lives the principles we are learning in this series is to memorize key scriptures. For many, memorization is a new concept or one that has been difficult in the past. We encourage you to stretch yourself and try to memorize these key verses. If possible, memorize them as a group and make them part of your group time. You may cut these apart and carry them in your wallet.

I have hidden your word in my heart that I might not sin against you.

Session One *Make a careful exploration of who you are and the work you have been given, and then sink yourself into that. Don't be impressed with yourself. Don't compare yourself with others. Each of you must take responsibility for doing the creative best you can with your own life.* Galatians 6:4–5 (MSG)	**Session Two** *God has given gifts to each of you from his great variety of spiritual gifts. Manage them well so that God's generosity can flow through you.* 1 Peter 4:10 (NLT)
Session Three *As a face is reflected in water, so the heart reflects the person.* Proverbs 27:19 (NLT)	**Session Four** *"His master replied, 'Well done, good and faithful servant! You have been faithful with a few things; I will put you in charge of many things. Come and share your master's happiness!'"* Matthew 25:23 (NIV)
Session Five *God works through different people in different ways, but it is the same God who achieves his purpose through them all.* 1 Corinthians 12:6 (PH)	**Session Six** *Praise be to the God and Father of our Lord Jesus Christ, the Father of compassion and the God of all comfort, who comforts us in all our troubles, so that we can comfort those in any trouble with the comfort we ourselves have received from God.* 2 Corinthians 1:3–4 (NIV)

NOTES

S.H.A.P.E.

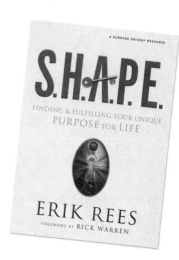

Rick Warren's bestselling book, *The Purpose Driven® Life,* described God's five purposes for every Christian. Now Erik Rees helps you discover God's unique purposes for your life based on the way God has shaped you. He made you marvelously unique for a reason. Tap into that reason and into the secrets of your own deeply personal makeup—the remarkable ensemble of passions, talents, experiences, temperament, and other components that work together to make you who you are—and you'll discover the path to a life of unimagined purpose, impact, and fulfillment.

In this eye-opening, empowering, and liberating book, Rees shows you how to uncover God's most powerful and effective means of advancing his kingdom on earth: your own irreplaceable, richly detailed personal design.

Based on the purpose of ministry outlined in *The Purpose Driven Life*, this inspiring guidebook gives you the tools to:

- Unlock your God-given potential
- Uncover your specific kingdom purpose
- Unfold a kingdom plan for your life

Filled with Scriptures and real-life stories, *S.H.A.P.E.* presents a series of challenges that will guide you through the process of discovering your S.H.A.P.E.—your personal blend of Spiritual Gifts, Heart, Abilities, Personality, and Experiences. You'll learn how to apply these attributes in ways that bring confidence, freedom, clarity, and significance that can only come from your Creator.

Your Life Review

Your Life Review is not a self-help, quick-fix, stop-the-pain-in-life experience. Rather it is a total life discovery and spiritual training process to help you refresh your spirit, refine your God-given S.H.A.P.E., and refocus your life on those things that matter most to God.

Your Life Review will guide you through the sequential Life Review & Response Process. It will enable you to gain a proper life perspective—above the noise and stress of the present burdens and requirements of life. From this vantage point, you can see God's love and hand in your life. You can find hope to face and resolve the pain and confusion from your past. You will catch a glimpse of your God-designed future, and begin to organize your life around the unique gifts and strengths God has given you.

The materials in the Your Life Review Planner are part of a course we offer at Saddleback Church, called Class 302—Your Life Review. This course was developed by Pastor Erik Rees, our Pastor of Ministry.

Your Life Review may be studied in one of two ways:

- In a small group or class format with a live presentation, using the Teacher's Kit and separate Participant's Workbooks. The Teacher's Kit includes: One printed copy of the Teacher's Workbook, four audio CDs of Pastor Erik's live presentations, one CD-ROM containing the lesson transcripts and PowerPoint® slides. (Note: Participant's Workbooks sold separately.)

- Self-guided study. You can go through this material at your own pace by using the Participant's Workbook and the four audio CDs of Pastor Erik's presentations (sold separately).

The Way of a Worshiper

The pursuit of God is the chase of a lifetime—in fact, it's been going on since the day you were born. The question is: Have you been the hunter or the prey?

This small group study is not about music. It's not even about going to church. It's about living your life as an offering of worship to God. It's about tapping into the source of power to live the Christian life. And it's about discovering the secret to friendship with God.

In these four video sessions, Buddy Owens helps you unpack the meaning of worship. Through his very practical, engaging, and at times surprising insights, Buddy shares truths from Scripture and from life that will help you understand in a new and deeper way just what it means to be a worshiper.

God is looking for worshipers. His invitation to friendship is open and genuine. Will you take him up on his offer? Will you give yourself to him in worship? Then come walk the Way of a Worshiper and discover the secret to friendship with God.

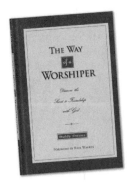

THE WAY of a WORSHIPER

Your study of this material will be greatly enhanced by reading the book,
*The Way of a Worshiper:
Discover the Secret to Friendship with God.*
